L E G A C I E S

SPORTS AND ENTERTAINMENT

Peter Hicks

Wayland

Legacies

Architecture
Clothes and Fashion
Language and Writing
Politics and Government
Science and Technology
Sports and Entertainment

Cover picture: Over 3,500 years ago, the Egyptians sailed on the River Nile with boats made of wood, like the one in the centre. Today, water is still vital for both trade and outdoor pursuits, such as windsurfing.

Series editor: Polly Goodman
Series designer: Liz Miller
Book designer: Malcolm Walker

First published in 1994 by
Wayland (Publishers) Limited
61 Western Road, Hove
East Sussex BN3 1JD, England

British Library Cataloguing in Publication Data
  Hicks, Peter
  Entertainment. – (Legacies Series)
  I. Title II. Bull, Peter III. Series
  790.09

ISBN 0 7502 1273 X

Typeset by Kudos Editorial and Design Services
Printed and bound in Italy by G.Canale & C.S.p.A., Turin

Contents

Legacies are things that are handed down from an ancestor or predecessor. The modern world has inherited many different legacies from ancient civilizations. This book explores the sports and entertainment legacies of the ancient world.

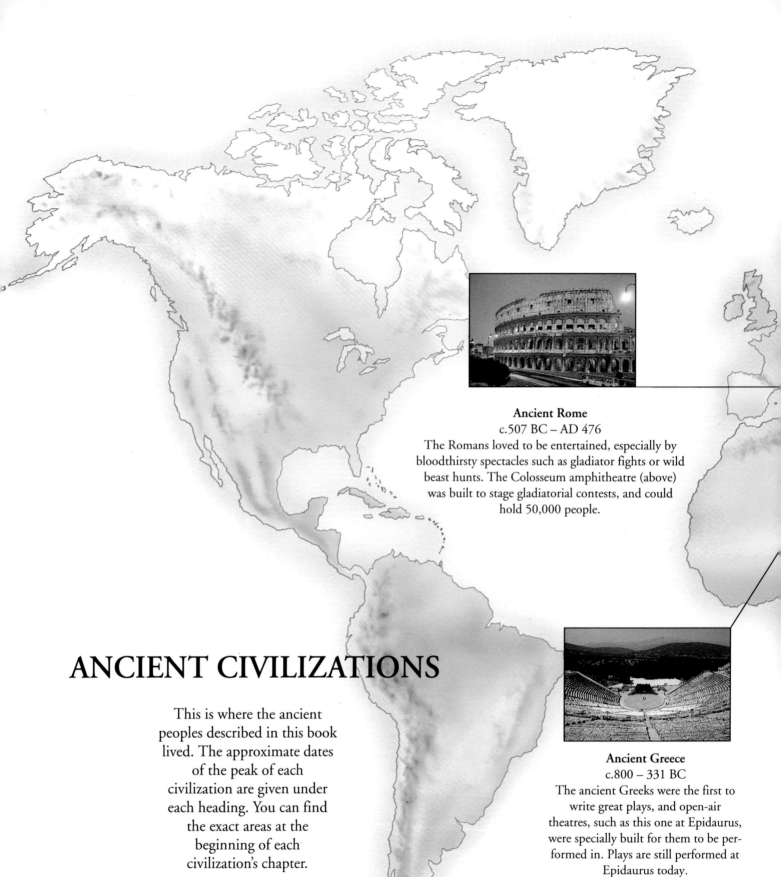

Ancient Rome
c.507 BC – AD 476
The Romans loved to be entertained, especially by bloodthirsty spectacles such as gladiator fights or wild beast hunts. The Colosseum amphitheatre (above) was built to stage gladiatorial contests, and could hold 50,000 people.

ANCIENT CIVILIZATIONS

This is where the ancient peoples described in this book lived. The approximate dates of the peak of each civilization are given under each heading. You can find the exact areas at the beginning of each civilization's chapter.

Ancient Greece
c.800 – 331 BC
The ancient Greeks were the first to write great plays, and open-air theatres, such as this one at Epidaurus, were specially built for them to be performed in. Plays are still performed at Epidaurus today.

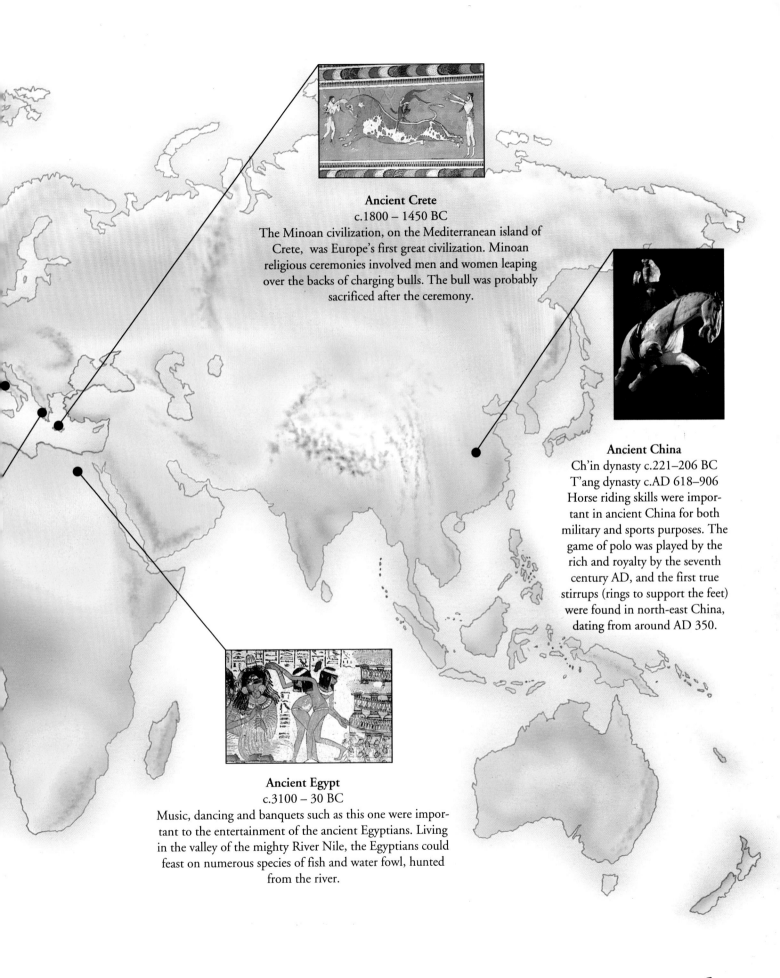

Ancient Crete
c.1800 – 1450 BC
The Minoan civilization, on the Mediterranean island of Crete, was Europe's first great civilization. Minoan religious ceremonies involved men and women leaping over the backs of charging bulls. The bull was probably sacrificed after the ceremony.

Ancient China
Ch'in dynasty c.221–206 BC
T'ang dynasty c.AD 618–906
Horse riding skills were important in ancient China for both military and sports purposes. The game of polo was played by the rich and royalty by the seventh century AD, and the first true stirrups (rings to support the feet) were found in north-east China, dating from around AD 350.

Ancient Egypt
c.3100 – 30 BC
Music, dancing and banquets such as this one were important to the entertainment of the ancient Egyptians. Living in the valley of the mighty River Nile, the Egyptians could feast on numerous species of fish and water fowl, hunted from the river.

chapter one

ENTERTAINMENT: MODERN AND ANCIENT

▼ *The University of Michigan Stadium in the USA is packed with spectators watching an American football game. Although we live in an age of mass-spectator sports, this scene would have been very familiar to the ancient Greeks and Romans.*

Entertainment today is an important way of relieving the stresses of modern life. People in developed countries have more leisure time now than in any time in history. What people do in this time is very important, be it hi-tech, home-based entertainment such as television, video or computer games, or mass-spectator sports such as soccer, American football or cricket. Watching a favourite television programme, cheering a sports team, or going to the cinema or theatre, are all popular ways of relaxing.

So it was in the past. In ancient times, the struggle against starvation made life and work hard, so any entertainment was a popular diversion. The rich, who were rulers, landowners, or merchants, tended to have more leisure time and therefore more access to entertainment. However, poorer people who lived in or near a town or city could see regular entertainments. Many ancient entertainments were similar to the hard and brutish life that some people lived. Many involved cruelty to other human beings and animals. Other sports involved running, jumping, chasing, throwing, aiming and prey-killing, which used hunting skills first used in the Stone Age. These skills are features of many modern team games and blood sports today. Many entertainments that we take for granted today have their roots in ancient civilizations. Their legacies have left a mark in the games, sport and cultural entertainments of the modern era.

▼ *This is the original stadium at Olympia in Greece, as it is today. The stadium is one 'stadion' long (192 m), which is where the word 'stadium' comes from. There were no seats for spectators, and the athletes entered the stadium through a tunnel off the bottom left of the picture. You can see the starting line and judges' box half-way down on the right.*

▼ *The ancient Greek theatre at Epidaurus has been restored to its original structure. It was built to hold 16,000 spectators and despite its size, even the people in the back row can hear sound clearly. The word 'theatre' comes from the Greek word 'theatron', meaning 'seeing place'.*

Every four years, millions of viewers all over the world watch the Olympic Games on television. Although there are many new sports in the modern Olympics, athletics, boxing and wrestling date back to the original Olympic Games, held in Greece in 776 BC. These Olympic Games, like today's, were held every four years. Dedicated to the god Zeus, they were taken very seriously. If any Greek states were at war with each other, the fighting had to stop so that their athletes could attend the five-day Games. The first modern Olympics were held in Athens in 1896, and were the idea of a Frenchman, Pierre de Coubertin. He wanted friendship to develop between young people from all over the world. He also wanted people to take part for the glory of winning and not for prizes or money. However, our modern Olympics have been criticized for drug scandals, political intrigue and money payments. We shall find out if the ancient Olympics were any different.

◄ *The layout of modern theatres and concert halls is very similar to that of ancient Greek theatres, such as Epidaurus. The tiered rows of seats, raised one above the other, mean that as many people as possible can see the stage. This is the Symphony Hall of the Birmingham International Conference Centre in England, which was built in 1992 to seat 2,200 people.*

Nowadays, there are theatres all over the world. Even in an age of television, a visit to the theatre to see a play is still very popular. Over 2,500 years ago, the Greeks had a thriving theatre. Ancient Greek theatre originated from a festival for the wine god, Dionysus. Singers and dancers, called a 'chorus', performed excerpts taken from the life of Dionysus. Original ancient Greek plays are often performed today, and we use Greek names for places in modern theatres, such as the 'orchestra' (from the Greek word meaning 'to dance'), which was and still is the place where the musicians and chorus performed.

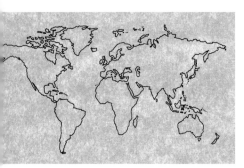

chapter two

ANCIENT
CRETE

▼ *This fresco shows the Minoan sport of bull leaping. To complete these leaps would need the agility of an Olympic gymnast together with the balance of a bareback rider!*

Between 2800 and 1150 BC, the ancient Minoan civilization grew and prospered on the island of Crete in the Mediterranean. It is called Minoan after one of its legendary kings, King Minos. King Minos is part of a famous legend about a monster, called a minotaur, who was half man and half bull. In the legend, the minotaur lived in a maze, or labyrinth, and each year ate fourteen young men and women from Athens. This was an offering to Crete from the city of Athens in Greece for losing an earlier war. When Theseus, son of the king of Athens, became one of the fourteen, he entered the labyrinth and finally killed the minotaur.

This story is a myth, but the bull was central to Minoan entertainment, respected for its strength, size and fertility. It was used in a daring and deadly game called bull leaping. Wall paintings called

frescos have been found, which show young men and women leaping and somersaulting over running bulls. It is believed that the athletes first grabbed the bull's horns, hoisted themselves above and through them, somersaulted, landed and bounced off the bull's back. Bull leaping was an

◄ *In the American rodeo, it is so dangerous for the rider that brightly coloured clowns are ready to distract the bull in case the rider falls. This clown is having trouble keeping out of the bull's way!*

extremely dangerous sport and the athletes risked a serious injury. Minoans also lassoed and wrestled bulls to the ground by their horns, just like cowboys and cowgirls do in the American rodeo today.

In the modern world, the bull is the centre of both Spanish bullfighting and the American rodeo. In Spanish bullfighting, men called banderillos and picadors wound the bull with banderillas (short, barbed, coloured staves), and lances, until it is weak. Then the matador, the bullfighter, dodges the bull's charges whilst trying to kill it with a sword. Before the fight begins, clowns perform acrobatic skills similar to those performed in Minoan bull leaping, somersaulting and cartwheeling in the arena to entertain the audience. In the American rodeo, the most dangerous event is bull riding. The riders, who can be men or women, have to stay on a jumping, twisting, kicking bull for eight seconds. These modern riders, like their ancient Minoan ancestors, have to combine strength and agility with courage.

▼ *During the July festival of San Fermin in Pamplona, Spain, hundreds of bulls are let loose through the town. Young men, wearing red neck ties, are chased down the streets to the bull ring. Other spectators have to scramble out of the way.*

BOXING

The Minoan civilization has the earliest references to boxing. Today, modern boxing, which is an Olympic sport, is beamed to millions of television screens all over the world. Many fights are long, bruising and violent exchanges, and boxers sometimes get seriously hurt or killed. Doctors have to be in attendance, and referees are supposed to stop the fight if one of the boxers has taken too much punishment.

► *This Minoan fresco from the sixteenth century BC shows two children boxing. We are not sure of the rules, but it is likely that slaps as well as punches were used.*

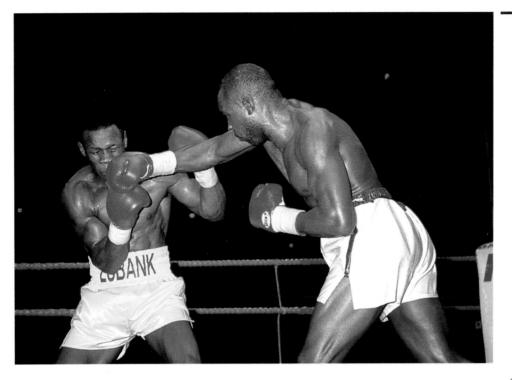

◀ *Modern world championship boxing is very popular with both spectators and gamblers, despite its brutality.*

▼ *The 'Boxer of Apollonius' is a later Greek bronze. You can see the protective leather thongs around his wrists and hands.*

Minoan boxers can be seen on ancient frescos and vases wearing helmets, like the leather helmets that modern boxers wear. Some Minoan boxers wore their hair loose in curls hanging down their backs. Like boxers today, Minoan boxers wore calf-high boots to strengthen their ankles while they ducked and weaved around their opponent. Around the midriff they wore loincloths or short kilts. To protect their fingers and knuckles, modern boxers have them taped together before putting on their boxing gloves. Minoan boxers also protected their fists, and they wore leather thongs over them which must have strengthened their punches. These may have been knuckle-dusters, metal guards slipped over the fingers to increase the damage of the blow. As some boxers wore bronze helmets, these might well have been necessary.

chapter three

ANCIENT EGYPT

6,000 years ago, ancient Egypt was a highly developed civilization. It thrived until 30 BC, when it was taken over by the Roman Empire. Water played an important part in the life of the ancient Egyptians. The mighty River Nile, which flows through Egypt, was known as the 'River of Life', bringing great fertility to the river valley each year, with its rich deposits of silt. Ancient Egyptian art, which decorated the insides of tombs and temples, shows that the River Nile was central to many forms of recreations in or on the water.

Mediterranean Sea

Nile Delta

R. Nile

EGYPT

KEY

☐ Area of fertile floodplain

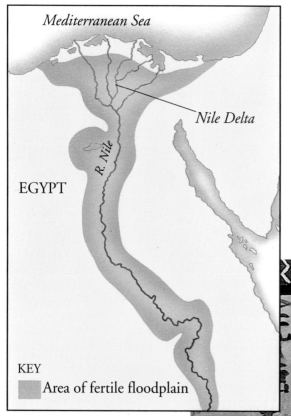

► In ancient Egypt, big boats were made of wood held together with wooden pegs and ropes. Smaller boats were made of bundles of reeds tied together, like the ones on page 17.

Today, watersports are a major form of entertainment. On the world's seas, rivers and lakes, you can often see swimmers, sailors, water-skiers, para-skiers, jet-skiers, surfers and windsurfers. Some people enjoy competing, while others enjoy watersports just for fun. Many people choose beach holidays with a warm climate because of the attraction of watersports.

▲ *Today, windsurfing is one of many sports which makes use of water for enjoyment. You can windsurf all over the world, on lakes or on the sea, as long as there is a good wind blowing.*

In ancient Egypt, many activities took place on the river, including sailing, trade and fishing. Being able to swim was a good idea in case there was an accident, but Egyptians also swam for pleasure. Wall paintings show women swimming under water to catch waterfowl, and a form of front crawl was taught. The front crawl, so different from the more natural doggy-paddle style of swimming, is now the fastest swimming style. Swimming lessons were compulsory for the households of Egyptian royalty and nobility. An ancient document tells how a nobleman was instructed by the Pharaoh 'to take swimming lessons along with the royal children'.

The Egyptians were excellent boat-builders, often using reeds, which grew in great abundance along the Nile, as their main building material. These boats were used in both work and play. Tomb frescos show young men in boats, armed with long poles, trying to push each other into the water. They also tried to tip their opponents' boat over. These games are very similar to competitions held today between lumberjacks in the Canadian logging games.

Rowing
Rowing was another popular watersport. The pharaohs celebrated with rowing festivals. At one, the pharaoh Amenophis II beat 200 other oarsmen.

▲ *These wrestlers are from an inscription in the Temple of Ramesses III in Egypt, which dates back to 1186 BC. Before each bout, the wrestlers would rub oil over their bodies to make it difficult for their opponent to grip them. The figure on the left is about to be thrown.*

WRESTLING

Some of the earliest references to wrestling can be found in ancient Egyptian art. Today, wrestling is very popular, mainly through the world-wide broadcasting of the World Wrestling Federation. Some wrestling personalities are known to millions of fans all over the world. An Egyptian tomb fresco gives a view of what wrestling was like about 4,000 years ago. Two figures, one painted brown and the other red, demonstrate over 120 different wrestling holds and throws. The sport was taken very seriously and it was professional then, just as it is today. Placards were carried with pictures of wrestling men on them which represented the wrestlers' profession like a badge.

FENCING

Besides wrestling, the ancient Egyptians enjoyed other competitive sports that involved fighting. One ancient

Egyptian sport was a kind of fencing that used sticks rather than swords. The stick was held in the right hand, while the left hand held a shield for protection. Some competitors wore helmets to protect their heads and faces. Sometimes mock battles took place with large numbers of fighters on both sides. One tomb fresco, dating from about 1160 BC, shows a stick fight between Egyptians, black Africans and a fighter from the Middle East. This may be the first recorded example of international competition. Ancient Egyptian team games included the 'Tug of War', which is still a popular game in many countries today. Alongside the pictures of these battles, there are comments such as 'My team is stronger than yours' and orders such as 'Hold fast comrades'.

▲ The crews of these papyrus rafts are mock fighting on their return from a hunting expedition. You can see the birds they have caught in a box. The boats are made of bundles of reeds, tied together.

◄ Modern fencing is so fast that the fencers have to wear pads wired up for electronic scoring. Hits are registered by a noise.

MUSIC

Music is put to many different uses today. At weddings, happy music celebrates a marriage; workers often play pop music in factories and workshops to help them work and discos play music you can dance to. Music was used in a similar way by the ancient Egyptians, who were great music lovers, particularly of strong rhythms.

▼ *In this banquet from around 1550 BC, the food is piled high in a colourful display on the right, while two young girls dance to the music of the double flute.*

The rich and leisured Egyptians demanded music throughout the day, especially during meals. A typical orchestra consisted of two flute players, two harpists, singers and clappers, although during huge religious or royal events, larger numbers of musicians were used. Women clappers, pipers and singers entertained farmers working in the fields and fishermen catching fish in the rivers. Music would have helped relieve the boredom of long hours of work. The rhythm might also have helped teams work well together, such as helping the fishermen pull in their nets in time with one another.

CHILDREN'S GAMES

Egyptian children in ancient times played speed and agility games just like those played in school playgrounds today. One was a high-jump game involving one child leaping over the joined feet and fingers of two others. Another game involved a child kneeling on the ground with one leg stretched out. The other players had to touch the child with their feet without being touched themselves. Whoever was caught had to take over on the ground. The evidence from Egyptian tombs and graves shows that ball games were also played. Some balls – which have been preserved and found today – were made of seamed, coloured leather, packed with straw or reeds. Other balls were wooden, like the ones thrown at coconut shies.

▲ *The origins of the harp*
Harps originated in ancient Egypt and they came in all shapes and sizes. Many were hand-held, others were played while kneeling, while some were as tall as the player and were played standing up. Egyptian harps had up to twenty strings.

▶ *The marshes of the Nile contained many species of waterfowl which were hunted by the ancient Egyptians, such as herons, geese and cormorants. This hunter, standing firmly in his boat, is about to launch a 'throw-stick' at the birds as they take off.*

HUNTING

Today, hunting takes place in many countries, although it is not as popular a form of entertainment as it used to be. Modern hunting includes shooting game or clay pigeons with high-velocity rifles or shotguns, and the more traditional fox-hunting on horseback. Before 5000 BC, hunting was an essential way of obtaining food. However, as societies gradually became based on farming, hunting also became a means of military training and a chance for leaders to impress their subjects. In ancient Egypt, pharaohs roamed the plains of the Upper Nile in their war chariots, in search of big game such as elephants, rhinoceroses, cattle and crocodiles. Their weapons were bows and arrows, lassos, spears and bolas (ropes which were 5 metres long with a stone attached to each end). When thrown at an animal, the bola wrapped itself around the animal's legs and slowed or brought it down. Ancient bolas are very similar to the bolas used against cattle on the plains of South America today.

Pharaohs liked to be seen by their peasants hunting hippopotamuses. The hippopotamuses could wreak havoc on crops around the Nile, and the peasants, who were not allowed to carry weapons, could do nothing about them. By keeping the hippopotamus numbers down, the pharaohs kept their popularity amongst their subjects, and were considered worthy kings and leaders. In modern politics, we often see this type of publicity to gain popularity. Political leaders like to have good press photos taken, especially when they are able to pose as leaders of action.

▲ *These hunters are looking for hippopotamuses in a papyrus swamp while a crocodile lurks under their raft.*

◄ *Modern hunting, with high-velocity rifles, is often just for entertainment. Pheasants, for example, are bred especially to be shot in the hunting season.*

chapter five

ANCIENT
GREECE

If you go to a play at the theatre, you may notice two masks on the programme. These are used as symbols for drama societies or film companies. One mask is happy, the other sad. These masks were used by the ancient Greeks in their plays, in a civilization which was at its peak between 800 – 331 BC. Masks were important in ancient Greek theatre for a number of reasons. They helped the audience to identify the characters easily. Since all the actors were male, they helped male actors to play female parts in a simple disguise. The masks also acted as loudspeakers, because the shape of the mouth helped sounds to travel much further. Finally, the expressions on the masks made it very clear to the audience how the characters were feeling.

Today's television includes situation comedies, thrillers and soap operas. Some make you laugh, some are exciting, and some make you sad. Ancient Greek theatre also produced a variety of plays. They were either comedies, tragedies or satires. Tragedies were serious plays and had sad endings. They often dealt with events drawn from myths, such as the terrible things that happened to the soldiers in the

▲ *These Greek theatre masks are copies of the original ancient masks. They have real hair attached to them and holes for the eyes and mouth.*

◄ *This is a modern performance of the Greek tragedy,* Oedipus Rex. *In the play, Oedipus, who is abandoned by his parents as a baby, grows up and marries his mother without knowing it. When he finds out, he blinds himself and his mother kills herself.*

legendary Trojan Wars of the twelfth century BC. Masks in these plays would look sad or tortured. Comedies, however, were full of jokes and had happy endings, while satires poked fun at serious topics. The masks in these plays were often smiling. The Greek comic dramatist Aristophanes, cleverly made fun of situations in everyday life, politicians or even the gods.

Modern theatre has inherited words from ancient Greek theatre. For example, the actors' changing room behind the orchestra was called a 'skene', which is where the modern word 'scene' comes from. Ancient Greek plays are often revived on modern stages. Aristophanes' play, *Lysistrata,* for example, was first performed in 411 BC, but it seems like a modern play. It concerns a group of women who try to prevent a war by stopping their husbands from fighting. The play's message of peace is very topical in the modern age. The play also seems modern in its positive portrayal of women, taking control of their lives and making decisions for themselves.

▼ *This Greek comic actor is impersonating a slave.*

OLYMPIC GAMES

Greece was the home of the original Olympics, which took place in 776 BC. The ancient Olympic Games were used by each Greek state to show off its wealth and status in competition with rival states. The athletes' training was also seen as a good preparation for war. Similar political rivalry between states is very common today. In 1980, when the Olympic Games were held in the former Soviet Union, the Russians tried to show their country in a good light. However, the United States and a number of other countries boycotted the Moscow Olympics as a protest against the Soviet Union's invasion of Afghanistan.

▼ *The Los Angeles Olympics in 1984 used 'Sam the Eagle' as the mascot of the Games, because the eagle is the symbol of the USA.*

▲ *In the 1988 Olympics in Seoul, South Korea, Ben Johnson appeared to have won the 100 m race. He was later stripped of his title, however, because he had cheated and had used drugs to win. Ancient Greek Olympians also tried to win by cheating.*

One of the most popular ancient events would never be allowed in the modern Olympics. The 'Pankration' event, from the Greek word meaning 'all-powerful', was a combination of wrestling, boxing and judo, but there were few rules and regulations. The fighters punched, elbowed, kicked, kneed and head-butted each other. The only form of aggression not allowed was the biting and gouging out of each other's eyes. Evidence shows that this was the most popular event!

Four years later, when the Olympics were held in Los Angeles, USA, it was the Soviet Union and its allied countries who boycotted the Games. The USA used the Olympics to show America off, and the opening ceremony was similar to a huge Hollywood musical. In the modern Olympic Games, the competition between countries trying to show off and appear better than others is very similar to the ancient Olympics.

Even in the ancient Olympics, heavy fines were imposed on athletes for bribery, cheating and lying. One athlete was fined for lying to the judges. He said he was late arriving at the Games because his ship had been delayed by bad weather, but witnesses saw him at another Games, winning prize money.

Dead Winner
In one Pankration event, the champion Arrachion died from strangulation just at the moment his opponent surrendered. The judges still crowned the dead Arrachion with the wreath and proclaimed him the winner.

25

▼ *These long-distance runners are on an ancient Greek vase, dating back to 470 BC. They are just about to turn around the turning post on the left.*

The fines collected from athletes paid for statues around the Olympic site, which served as a warning to cheats. Athletes who appeared in the Olympic Games also travelled to other games, where they could win cash prizes. When an athlete brought great fame to his home town, he was sometimes granted free meals for life. This is not very different from today's athletes, who compete all over the world and are sometimes paid generous appearance money, or win television advertising contracts.

At first, the ancient Olympic Games consisted only of running races. Other events were introduced later, however. The athletes had to compete completely naked and barefoot. This rule was later applied to the trainers of the athletes as well, after an incident concerning an athlete's

◄ The Olympic flame is a symbol inherited from the original Games, held in Olympia, Greece, in 776 BC. In the ancient Games, which were part of a religious ceremony, young men raced to light a sacrificial fire. The sacrifice was made in honour of the goddess Rhea, 'Mother of Gods'. Today, every modern Olympic site burns the flame, which is lit by a torch carried from Olympia in Greece.

mother. Women were not allowed as spectators to the games, so one mother, who wanted to see her son compete in the boxing event, disguised herself as a man and pretended to be her son's trainer. When her son won however, she leapt over a barrier in her excitement and, as her disguise fell off, gave herself away. After this, a rule was brought in that all trainers must go as naked as the athletes.

► Sports Centres

The ancient Greeks were building sports centres by the third century BC. The Great Gymnasium and Palaestra (athletics hall) in Olympia provided a covered running track and wrestling ground where Olympic athletes could train in bad weather.

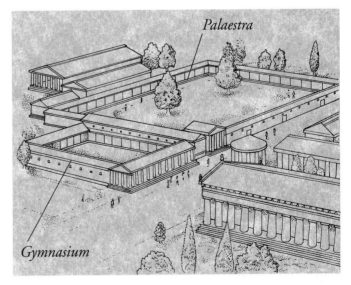

Palaestra

Gymnasium

► *These clay models show two ladies playing the game* Pentalitha, *or knucklebones. They are holding the joints of animal bones, which were the game pieces. The game depended on chance, on how the bones landed after they were thrown.*

▼ *Roulette is a modern game which depends on chance, just like the ancient Greek game of* Pentalitha. *In roulette, players make bets on where the ball will stop before throwing it into the spinning roulette wheel.*

INDOOR GAMES

Apart from the great Olympic event, there were other entertainments, especially for children and wealthy women. In the modern game of *Jacks*, angular pieces of metal have to be picked up in the time it takes for a ball to bounce. The game originated from the ancient Greek game called *Pentalitha*, meaning knucklebones, because the original pieces used were the joints of animal bones. *Kollabismos* was a Greek version of the modern *Blind Man's Bluff*. A blindfolded player was smacked by an other player and had to find out who it was. *Askoliasmos* was a messier version of the modern game *Twister*, where the players had to stand and balance on a wineskin covered in olive oil. Children's toys found in ancient Greek tombs consist of small clay figures riding horses and other animals. They are not so different from the plastic or metal figures for children today.

MUSIC

Music and song were an important part of Greek birth, marriage and funeral ceremonies, just as they are to modern ceremonies. Instruments such as the lyre, harp, flute and panpipes were played. All the events at the Olympic Games – apart from running – were accompanied by pipe and flute playing.

◄ *This ancient Greek vase shows Terpsichore, the goddess of dance and song, playing the harp. She is surrounded by women playing the double flute and the lyre. Although hardly any evidence of Greek music has survived, we know that it was central to everyday life. Even Greek hoplites (warriors) were accompanied by flute playing as they advanced into battle.*

chapter six

ANCIENT
ROME

The great spectator sports of the modern world thrive on big occasions such as the Super Bowl, the European Cup Final and the World Cup. During these events, huge stadia containing over 100,000 people each are packed with spectators, and television cameras send pictures of the matches to televisions all over the world. Huge stadia were pioneered by the ancient Romans between c.507 BC – AD 476, and in them they staged contests, races and games. They were so obsessed by their games that it was often said that the citizens of Rome were only interested in entertainment and food. In Rome itself, two huge monuments to entertainment were built: the Colosseum for gladiatorial contests, which held 50,000 people, and the Circus Maximus, a specially designed course for chariot racing, which held 200,000 people.

In 1993, the television game show *Gladiators* brought gladiators into modern entertainment. In the game show, modern gladiators took part in physical contests with members of the public. There was a 'race to the death' at the end of the programme. Roman gladiators were

▲ *In this model of Imperial Rome, you can see the circular Colosseum in the centre and the oval-shaped Circus Maximus in the foreground. The island in the middle of the Circus Maximus was known as the 'Spina' and the charioteers had to race around this in an anti-clockwise direction.*

extremely popular fighters. The games are thought to have originated from the Roman belief that it was necessary to spill human blood at funerals, to prevent the souls of the dead coming back to haunt the living. At first, slaves were ordered to fight and passers-by were charged to watch and take a seat. This was how the gladiatorial contest was born. The gladiators were slaves who were sent to special training schools to be taught the art of fighting. Roman audiences loved to see fights between different types of gladiators. Some were armed with short swords and small shields, while others fought with a spear and a net. If a gladiator's performance had not pleased the spectators, they would condemn him to death. Some gladiators survived many fights, became famous, and bought their freedom.

▲ *These modern 'gladiators' are only mock fighting in this television game show, using plastic hammers instead of swords. They, like their Roman predecessors, wear protective helmets.*

▲ *These Roman gladiators are fighting to the death with swords in a test of strength and skill.*

Mad Caligula
The games were used by the Romans to execute enemies and criminals. However, during Emperor Caligula's reign (AD 37– 41), he was so angry when there were no prisoners to kill that he decided to throw a crowd of spectators into the arena to be slaughtered by wild beasts.

► *These soldiers are killing leopards for the entertainment of an important Roman called Magerius. The soldiers are paid 1,000 denarii each for this, which Magerius's servant brings out in bags on a tray.*

▲ *Bullfighting in Spain is a controversial blood sport today, just as the Games were in Roman times. The bull, weakened by the banderillas in his neck, is about to be slaughtered by a matador with a sword, just visible under the red cape.*

BLOOD SPORTS

Animals were brought from all over the Roman Empire to fight with gladiators in specially built arenas called amphitheatres. Hundreds of thousands of animals were killed in this way. Just as many people today have strong feelings against blood sports, so it was in Roman times. The great orator Cicero wrote about his doubts to a friend: ' . . . what pleasure can it possibly be to a man of culture whether a human being is ripped apart by a powerful beast, or a splendid beast is killed with a spear.'

RATINGS

Just as television networks today compete to think up the most popular shows, ratings were important in the Roman games. New and impressive spectacles had to be displayed to attract people. Sometimes an aqueduct was fed into the amphitheatre so that sea-battles could be re-enacted.

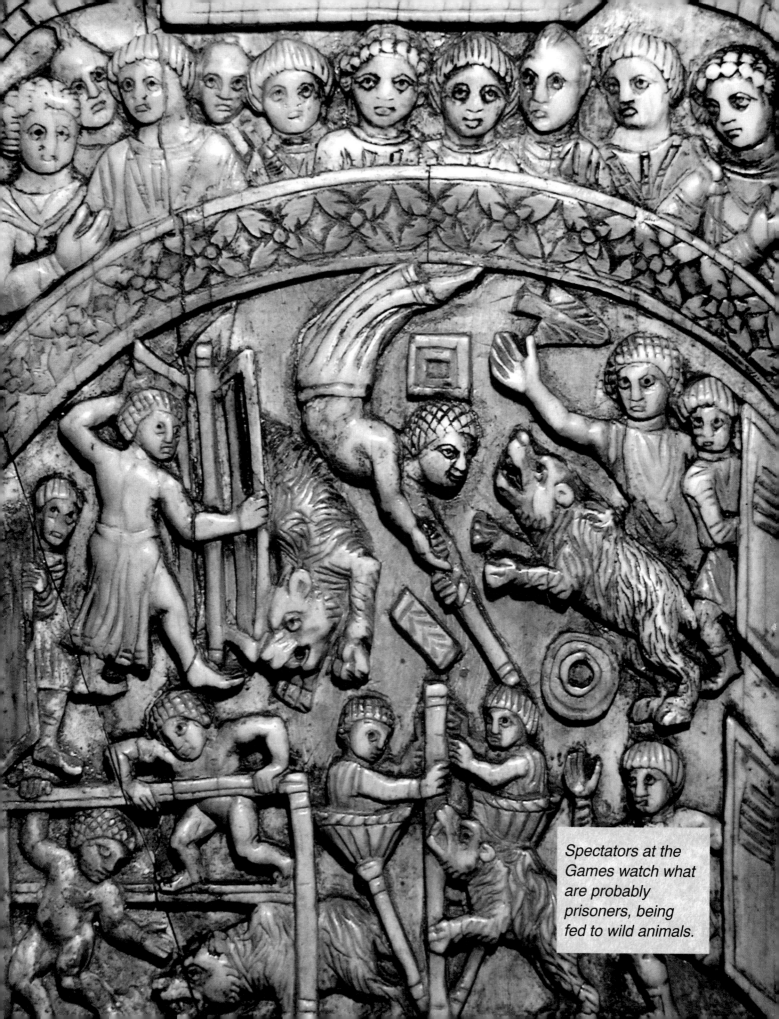

Spectators at the Games watch what are probably prisoners, being fed to wild animals.

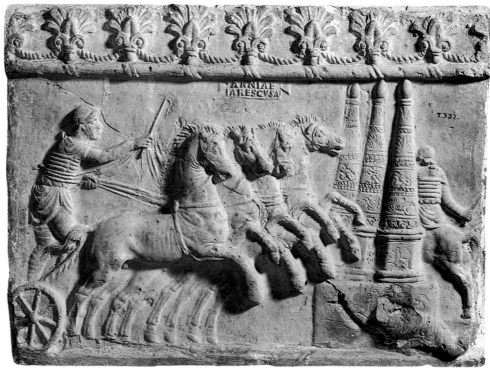

▶ *This four-horse chariot is approaching the three columns of the turning post. Chariot races were a mass of confusion, dust and noise. The course was seven laps of the track, and each day could contain up to twenty races.*

Sports mad
Nero (AD 54–68) was so fanatical about the chariot races that when his wife Poppaea complained about his late return from them, he murdered her!

RACING

Throughout history, people have wanted to drive their vehicles as fast as possible. The fastest four-wheeled vehicles today can be seen on the Indy Car and Grand Prix circuits. You can often see the winners wearing laurel wreaths while spraying their huge bottles of champagne, and some motor racing teams and tyre companies use the laurel wreath in their advertising. The laurel wreath is a legacy from Greek and Roman times, when wreaths were awarded to the champions of chariot races. Chariot racing was very popular amongst the Greeks, and the Romans made it into a favourite mass-spectator sport. Like the Indy Car and Grand Prix circuits, the charioteers formed teams, known as factions: Blue, Green, White and Red. The charioteers were often slaves or from the poorer classes, but if they won they could become very famous. They could then go to the faction that offered them the greatest amount of money. Chariot racing was a very dangerous sport, which is one of the reasons why so many people watched it. During the high-speed races, the charioteers tried to smash their chariot into their opponent's, hoping to destroy it. If this happened it was known as shipwrecking, and the charioteer had to cut the reins or be violently dragged to a certain death. Today, the sport of trotting is a less violent version of chariot racing. In trotting, single horses pull two-wheeled vehicles in a race around a track. The horse can only trot because the chariot is attached very closely behind, whereas in ancient Roman chariot racing, four horses were able to gallop freely.

HOOLIGANISM

Hooliganism is often thought to be the result of modern times, particularly surrounding football. However, violence between team supporters dates right back to the followers of ancient chariot factions. Support for the Blues and the Greens was fanatical. Followers were obsessed by their favourite drivers and their colour. In the eastern Roman Empire's capital, Constantinople, rioting fans burnt down the wooden arena for chariot racing five times before the emperor replaced it with a stone one. The worst riot was in AD 532, when the Green and Blue factions joined together in a riot. The army was called in and an estimated 30,000 people were killed.

▲ *This charioteer is wearing the racing colours of his sponsor, just as racing jockeys today wear the colours of their horse owner. He wears a protective leather helmet. Modern jockeys wear harder helmets called skull caps.*

◄ *The modern sport of trotting is the nearest we have to chariot racing today. Trotting is very popular in Australia, the USA and many countries in Europe.*

SPORTS CENTRES

Sports centres are very popular in modern times. They are used for activities such as swimming, squash and work-outs, and for saunas, jacuzzis and solariums. 2,000 years ago, the Roman baths provided similar facilities. Roman towns and cities had at least one public bath, which provided many attractions other than bathing. They were important meeting places and often became the social centre of the town. Apart from bathing, the baths provided

► *The Roman Baths in Bath, England, are still well-preserved today. Special underground heating systems called 'hypocausts' made bathers sweat and their skin pores open. Once the sweat was scraped off, bathers took hot or cold plunge baths.*

◄ *Large indoor swimming pools, like this water park in Alberta, Canada, are popular places to spend leisure time, just as the bath houses were in the Roman Empire.*

gymnasia, bowling alleys, wine bars, snack bars and reading rooms. It was quite common to work out in the gym, before cleaning up in a bath, and enjoying a glass of wine with a snack. The baths were highly organized, and the larger ones could cater for thousands of people. They were reasonably priced so that most people could afford them.

▼ *Romans relaxed in bars like this one, from AD 100 in Ostia, Italy. Ostia was the port for Rome.*

Today, a popular way of relaxing for adults is to go to the local bar or pub. They are more than just places to buy drinks; they provide music, company, food, entertainment and comfortable surroundings. The Romans enjoyed this form of relaxation too. The Roman city of Pompeii, destroyed by a volcano in AD 79, had no less than 120 wine bars.

chapter seven

ANCIENT CHINA

HORSES

Horses today are used in many sports and entertainments including polo, racing and show jumping. Polo, which originated in Persia, was being played in China by the seventh century AD. Like the game today, two teams of riders used their mallets to try and hit a wooden ball through their opponents' goal posts. Sometimes the game was more like a target practice than a competition between teams. The mallets they used resembled the clubs used

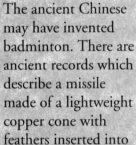

Badminton
The ancient Chinese may have invented badminton. There are ancient records which describe a missile made of a lightweight copper cone with feathers inserted into it – the first shuttlecock.

▶ *This impressive model of an ancient Chinese polo player shows all the movement and strength of his horse. Notice that his arm position is very similar to that of a sword blow – polo was good training for the warrior class of ancient China.*

◀ *Modern polo can be fast and dangerous for both the rider and the horse.*

by hunters on horseback. The game required expert horse skills and it became a fashionable sport played by both men and women. Since horses were expensive to keep and train, just as they are today, the sport was played mainly by royalty and the rich.

▼ *This modern golfer could be playing a game that is over 2,000 years old.*

GOLF

Golf is another popular modern sport, with new golf courses opening frequently. Golf tournaments, such as the American Masters, have a huge following and are given lengthy television coverage. In China, a form of golf called *Wan-Chin* was being played by the sixth century AD. A manual, written in that century explains the rules of *Wan-Chin*, describing the ball, clubs, fouls, number of players and conditions of the course. The manual warns that the game was only suitable for gentlemen, which was also the early attitude of British golfers. Many ancient Chinese officials and politicians found the game so enjoyable that they disregarded their public duties in order to play.

The Yin and Yang
that the poet Lu Yu
referred to is a
traditional belief of
the Chinese. They
believed that forces
should perfectly
balance each other.
Yang represents light,
summer and warmth,
while Yin represents
darkness, winter
and cold.

FOOTBALL

One of the most popular sports in history is football.
The earliest recorded evidence of a game resembling
football is in China. The game, played in northern China
from at least the third century BC, did not allow players to
use their arms, so that their feet would keep warm. The
game was referred to as *tsu chu*, *tsu* meaning 'to kick with
the foot', and *chu* meaning 'the stuffed leather ball'.
There was even poetry written about *tsu chu*. The poet Lu
Yu (AD 1125–1210) hung his poetry on the goal posts,
similar to the banners which supporters bring into football
stadiums today, praising their favourite players. Here is one
of Yu's ancient poems:

> 'A round ball and a square goal
> suggest the shape of Yin and the Yang.
> The ball is like the full moon
> and the two teams stand opposed;
> captains are appointed and take their place'

Yu's words show how seriously the Chinese took the game:

> 'Determination and coolness are essential
> and there must not be the slightest irritation for failure.
> Such is the game. Let its principles apply to life.'

▶ *Banners and flags
are an important part
of the football
tradition. These
Brazilian fans, whose
team has just won the
1970 World Cup held
in Mexico, support
their team with
banners, drums and
smoke bombs.*

◀ *Archery is a legacy from ancient China. The Chinese developed the composite bow between AD 400–500. These first bows were made of thin strips of wood that were laminated with animal sinew, giving them double the tension and fire-power of ordinary bows of a similar weight.*

▼ **Wrestling**
Like the Egyptians, the ancient Chinese were wrestling over 2,000 years ago. This bronze statuette is from between the fourth and the third centuries BC.

ARCHERY

Archery is a popular sport today, with thousands of participants all around the world. Modern bows are hi-tech machines, made with complicated sights and balances. In ancient China, archery was of great importance to warriors. Chinese warriors practised constantly, trying to pierce fabric and metal with specially prepared, heavy arrows. Archery was also used by the peasantry to hunt for food to supplement their diet. The upper classes held exclusive competitions where the participants, all beautifully dressed, fired one arrow in front of, one behind, and one from the side of a charging horse.

THEATRE AND FESTIVALS

Chinese theatre started in ancient times as a mobile tradition of acrobatics and song. Chinese circus and opera troupes travelled from city to city to put on their performances, a tradition popular with the emperors of China. Performers jumped, tumbled and juggled with tables, ropes, hoops, balls, clubs and knives, entertaining people in streets and market-places. Modern Chinese circuses are still famous for their acrobats and jugglers, and Western theatre companies and circuses travel on the road in a similar way. The ancient Chinese troupes were invited

▶ *Chinese festivals are still celebrated according to the lunar calendar today, especially by Chinese communities living in Western cities, such as the Chinatowns of Vancouver in Canada, San Francisco in the USA, and London in England. Like the theatre, Chinese festivals use exotic costumes and make-up.*

◀ *This Chinese opera, performed in Penang, Malaysia, uses brilliant scenery and extravagant costume.*

▼ *The ancient Chinese discovered gunpowder and created spectacular fireworks. Modern cities often celebrate special occasions with a firework display, such as this one on Sydney Harbour in Australia on New Year's Eve.*

to festivals, which were related to the lunar calendar. These festivals included the New Year and Midsummer festivals, and those of the August and September moons, which celebrated the harvest and selling of crops. In these festivals, which are still celebrated today, villages and towns competed to hire the most famous and expensive troupes. This still happens between towns in modern arts festivals today. Ancient Chinese theatre is famous for its exotic costume, bright make-up and loud music. The make-up, like the masks in ancient Greek theatre, made it easy for the audience to recognize characters. The make-up also helped the male actors play female parts because, as in Greek theatre, women were not allowed on the stage. Gongs, kettle drums and numerous wind instruments interrupted the actors' voices and the audiences responded loudly to jokes, just like modern audiences in television situation comedies, or the audiences of stand-up comedians.

Ancient Greece and Crete

Before 3000 B.C.	2000 B.C.	1000 B.C.	0	A.D.

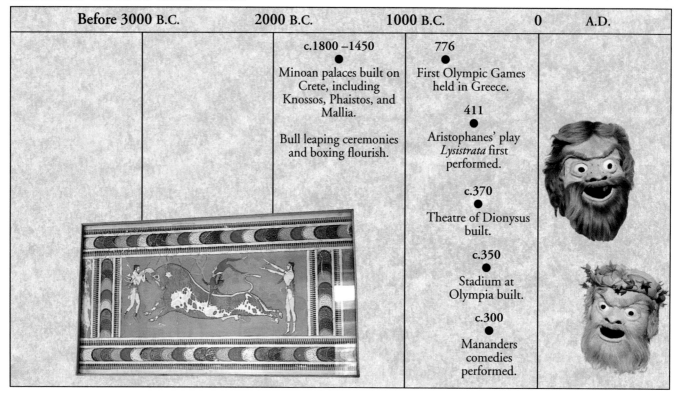

c.1800–1450
●
Minoan palaces built on Crete, including Knossos, Phaistos, and Mallia.

Bull leaping ceremonies and boxing flourish.

776
●
First Olympic Games held in Greece.

411
●
Aristophanes' play *Lysistrata* first performed.

c.370
●
Theatre of Dionysus built.

c.350
●
Stadium at Olympia built.

c.300
●
Mananders comedies performed.

Ancient Rome

Before 3000 B.C.	2000 B.C.	1000 B.C.	0	A.D.

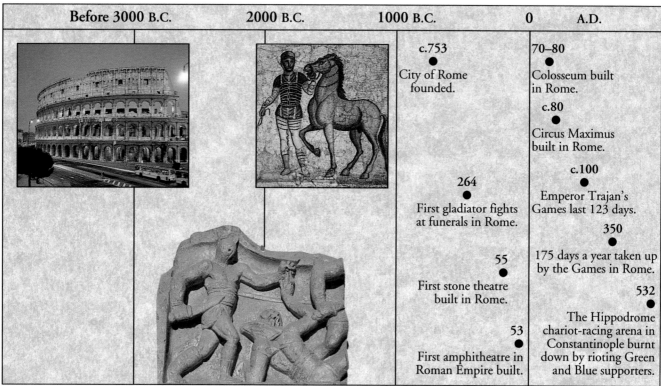

c.753
●
City of Rome founded.

264
●
First gladiator fights at funerals in Rome.

55
●
First stone theatre built in Rome.

53
●
First amphitheatre in Roman Empire built.

70–80
●
Colosseum built in Rome.

c.80
●
Circus Maximus built in Rome.

c.100
●
Emperor Trajan's Games last 123 days.

350
●
175 days a year taken up by the Games in Rome.

532
●
The Hippodrome chariot-racing arena in Constantinople burnt down by rioting Green and Blue supporters.

Ancient China

Before 3000 B.C.	2000 B.C.	1000 B.C.	0	A.D.

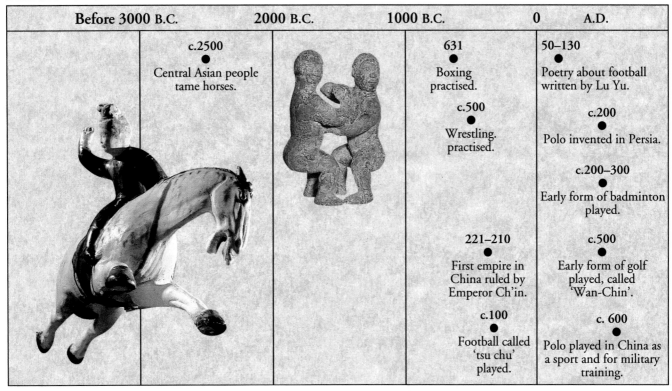

c.2500
●
Central Asian people tame horses.

631
●
Boxing practised.

c.500
●
Wrestling. practised.

221–210
●
First empire in China ruled by Emperor Ch'in.

c.100
●
Football called 'tsu chu' played.

50–130
●
Poetry about football written by Lu Yu.

c.200
●
Polo invented in Persia.

c.200–300
●
Early form of badminton played.

c.500
●
Early form of golf played, called 'Wan-Chin'.

c. 600
●
Polo played in China as a sport and for military training.

Ancient Egypt

Before 3000 B.C.	2000 B.C.	1000 B.C.	0	A.D.

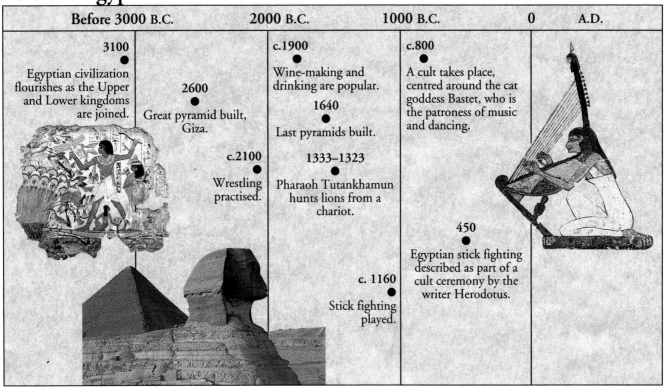

3100
●
Egyptian civilization flourishes as the Upper and Lower kingdoms are joined.

2600
●
Great pyramid built, Giza.

c.2100
●
Wrestling practised.

c.1900
●
Wine-making and drinking are popular.

1640
●
Last pyramids built.

1333–1323
●
Pharaoh Tutankhamun hunts lions from a chariot.

c. 1160
●
Stick fighting played.

c.800
●
A cult takes place, centred around the cat goddess Bastet, who is the patroness of music and dancing.

450
●
Egyptian stick fighting described as part of a cult ceremony by the writer Herodotus.

GLOSSARY

Aqueduct   A bridge for carrying water above ground.

Blood sports   Sports which involve the killing of animals.

Boycotted   Deliberately avoided.

Bribery   The giving or taking of secret gifts with the intention of doing something dishonest or illegal.

Chariot   An open, two-wheeled vehicle pulled by horses.

Charioteers   Chariot drivers.

Developed countries   Countries that have a high standard of living based on industry and trade.

Fanatical   To feel extremely strongly about something.

Fertility   The ability of land to produce seeds or plants, or people to have children.

Frescos   Paintings made on walls covered in fresh, damp plaster.

Gladiators   Men, usually slaves, who were specially trained to fight to the death in Roman public arenas.

Hollywood   An area in Los Angeles in California, USA, where films are made.

Hooliganism   Outbreaks of lawlessness by gangs.

Lassoed   Caught with a long rope with a loop at the end.

Laurel wreaths   The leaves of a laurel shrub made into a garland, usually in a ring shape.

Leisure time   Free time when people are not working.

Mallets   Wooden hammers.

Myths   Made-up stories about heroes or gods of ancient times.

Nobility   The class or group of nobles, people of high rank in a country.

Pharoah   An Egyptian king.

Political intrigue   The scheming of people to get advantage over others.

Rodeo   A competitive sport, usually in North America, where contestants display the skills of cowboys, bareback riding and rounding up cattle.

Stone Age   The period before 6000 BC when stone was used for tools and weapons.

Stadia   Large, open-air sports grounds with rows of seats for spectators to watch events.

Thongs   Strips of leather which are used for fastening.

Trojan Wars   Legendary conflicts between Greece and the city of Troy, in what is today known as Turkey.

Waterfowl   Birds which live on or near the water.

BOOKS TO READ

Civilizations of Asia by Brian Williams (Ed.) (Cherry Tree Books, 1990)
Civilizations of the Middle East by Brian Williams (Ed.) (Cherry Tree Books, 1992)
The Atlas of Ancient Worlds by A. Millard (Dorling Kindersley, 1994)
The Atlas of the Ancient World by Margaret Oliphant (Ebury Press, 1992)
The Dark Ages by Tony Gregory (Simon & Schuster, 1991)
The Earliest Civilizations by Margaret Oliphant (Simon & Schuster, 1991)
The History of Europe by Brian Dicks (Wayland, 1992)

Picture acknowledgements:
The publishers would like to thank the following for allowing their pictures to be used in this book:
Action Plus 13 (top); All-Sport (UK) Ltd 24 (top & bottom); Ancient Art & Architecture Collection 12, 22, 44 (top right); C M Dixon 7, 13 (bottom), 21 (top), 23 (top & bottom), 28 (top), 30, 31 (bottom), 32 (top), 33, 35 (top), 37 (bottom), 41 (bottom), 44 (bottom & middle), 45 (top right); Eye Ubiquitous 11 (bottom), 35 (bottom), 42, 43 (bottom); Sonia Halliday 4, 10, 44 (top left); Robert Harding 4, 8-9, 11 (top), 32 (bottom), 36; Images Colour Library 6-7; London Weekend Television 31 (top); Michael Holford *Cover (inset)*, 14, 20, 25, 26, 29, 34, 45 (bottom left); Tony Stone Worldwide *Cover (main)*, 5, 15, 17 (bottom), 37 (top), 39 (top & bottom), 40, 41 (top), 44 (bottom left); Wayland Picture Library 43 (top); Werner Forman Archive 4, 5, 16, 17 (top), 18, 19, 38, 44 (top left & bottom right); Zefa 9, 21 (bottom), 27, 28 (bottom). All artwork is by Peter Bull.

INDEX

Numbers in **bold** refer to illustrations.